How to Make BIG BUCKS from BIG BLOGS

By Brandon Colker

Table of Contents

Introduction

There's an old episode of The Simpsons in which Homer, after discovering his neighbor has started a successful business using the Internet, decides to start an online business of his own. Homer's impetuousness and impatience leads him to immediately set up a home office -- complete with a typewriter instead of a computer -- expecting the money to just roll in without any effort whatsoever. Well, not without any effort whatsoever, as he does consult a book (Internet for Dummies: Remedial Edition) and seeks Marge's advice for naming his business, which she brilliantly dubs Compu-Global-Hyper-Mega-Net.

When Homer tells his wife, "Everybody's making money off the Internet except us. We've fallen behind. WAY behind," his statement and the actions that follow illustrate several common misconceptions about generating income through the Internet, many of which still exist nearly 20 years after that episode first aired. There is money to be made through online blogging, but it takes a lot of work and requires a significant investment of time and energy to be successful. Homer's haphazard and ill-informed approach is not uncommon, and failure is all but assured without proper planning and preparation.

I hope you can forgive my example, as there is

probably a better way to illustrate a point than making reference to the "B" plot of a cartoon that first aired in 1998. Unfortunately, a lot of Homer's behavior in that episode reminded me of my own when I first began. Of course, I knew better than to try to connect to the Internet using a typewriter, but I did believe that starting a blog and using it as a primary source of income required very little effort and would be immediately lucrative. I made a lot of mistakes on the way to achieving my current level of success, but I would have saved myself from a great deal of frustration had I better prepared myself when I first began.

Essentially, the information included in this book represents the advice I would give the Brandon Colker of 15 years ago if it were possible to go back and do so. Clearly, that is not the case, but it is my hope that I can help others who are just starting out by sharing the many lessons I have learned over the years. This will include everything from general writing practice to specific passive income strategies, with the advice specifically geared toward the beginning blogger. While this is a book intended to assist those who are just starting out, I still believe that there is a great deal of advice I have to offer that will be beneficial to veteran bloggers as well.

It is of the utmost importance that you recognize that while there is a lot of hard work involved -- especially when you first start out -- the eventual payoff is incredibly rewarding. There are no shortcuts to success when it comes to building the kind of blog that eventually becomes the foundation of a passive income empire, but having a plan of action that outlines a clear path to success will help in expediting the process while revealing all of the potential pitfalls that may lie ahead. So whether you are already an expert in your field or you are still trying to establish yourself as one, the chapters that follow are intended to help you on your way so that you are able to share your vast expertise while making money for doing so.

"Big Blogs, Big Bucks," includes 10 chapters, and I promise that any other silly pop culture references appearing in the pages that follow are absolutely necessary to make an important point or are somehow essential. I have made every effort to be as thorough as possible in elucidating every aspect of blogging for passive income, but I have also endeavored to be concise as frequently as possible. After all, anyone reading this book is probably quite excited to get started on the processes I have outlined, so it is my hope that the relative brevity of the chapters is to the benefit of the reader, as I have tried to stuff each one with only the most useful and relevant information.

The book begins with an introduction to blogging for passive income and closes with chapters that discuss how to put all the principles I have outlined into practice. It is my goal that, after completing this book, you will have a deep understanding of how to start a blog from scratch and how to build it into an unstoppable passive income machine that is the favorite bookmark of your eager readers.

An Introduction to Passive Income Through Blogging

Surely you have heard about passive income at some point, and it is fairly likely that you have heard it described in the kind of terms that make generating income in this way seem incredibly easy. I recall speaking to a friend about it some time ago, and he made it seem as though earning passive income was a snap: After just a bit of effort on our part, we could just sit back and wait for the big checks to show up week after week. It wasn't true then, and it isn't true today. Passive income requires active effort when you are first starting out, and only when a blog is properly established is it possible to earn a solid and consistent income.

Before beginning a blog in earnest, it is important to understand precisely what passive income means, just as it is important to recognize that those who now count on the passive income generated by their blog as a primary source of income are able to do so because they focused on laying a solid foundation first. In this chapter, I will offer a clear and concise definition of passive income while also answering the following questions, all of which I believe are central to gaining an understanding of passive income strategies:

- How does a blog generate passive income?
- Why is it important to make such a significant time investment up front?
- How do bloggers set reasonable goals and expectations?
- Why is it important to establish trust, and what are the consequences of breaking that trust?

What Is Passive Income?

Before I touch on each of those subjects, allow me to first offer a definition that will clarify what I am talking about each time I use the term "passive income." To me, passive income is any income generated by an online business that uses automated systems for bringing in consistent cash flow. This type of income is called "passive" because there is no need for your presence for any transaction to take place; it happens automatically. This extends not just to payments, as your business should be able to grow without your active presence, allowing you to move on to creating new opportunities for generating additional passive income. Essentially, almost all of your efforts should be completed at the outset, allowing you to reap a continual reward for work that you have already completed.

How Does a Blog Generate Passive Income?

There are many methods blogs can use to generate

passive income, and I have devoted all of Chapter 8 to providing in-depth explanations of each of those methods and the various benefits they provide. Without going into much detail here, bloggers can use advertising, sponsorships and affiliate marketing, along with the sale of books, seminars, training sessions, speaking engagements and more. Each of these methods is deserving of in-depth analysis, and comprehensive explanations are provided in Chapter 8.

The Necessity of an Initial Time Investment

The whole point of establishing sources of passive income is to avoid committing a great deal of time to actively working, so many bloggers are understandably hesitant to accept the initial time requirement involved. In all honesty, I was one of those bloggers, and there is no reason to feel bad about wanting more free time to enjoy all the world has to offer. Simply understand that the initial time investment will yield a much more significant return when a blog is set up properly. It is of paramount importance to offer your readers products and services that are worth their hard-earned money, so make sure that what you initially create is the product of great care and honest effort.

Setting Reasonable Expectations and Goals

I am all but certain that there are multiple examples

of bloggers who could be considered "overnight sensations," but these examples would represent the exception, not the rule. Establishing a blog that generates significant passive income takes time, and patience is necessary in this regard. Even after you have successfully laid a strong foundation, it is foolhardy to immediately expect six-figure monthly revenues. With solid products and services, however, your reputation will eventually grow at an exponential rate, ultimately reaching a point where such sizable revenues are indeed a possibility. Setting incremental goals and taking steps to achieve those goals will make the process more enjoyable while making it more likely that long-term goals are realized.

Importance of Establishing Trust

Unfortunately, there are many ways that bloggers can take advantage of people. Even if you have no intention of engaging in this type of behavior, it is important to recognize that there is a general wariness that you may have to contend with, so establishing and maintaining a strong sense of trust with your readers is of the utmost importance. Commit to being transparent whenever possible and never engage in the sort of behavior that could be viewed as underhanded, as you must do everything within your power to always protect your good reputation.

Outlining the Appropriate Use of Branding and Self-Promotion

Building the initial foundation for a blog that generates passive income requires a certain level of self-promotion and the establishment of a clearly identifiable brand. This may seem unappealing to some, and while it is certainly possible that a blog can become wildly profitable in a more organic way, it is simply the case that bloggers who are willing to promote their expertise while establishing a clear identity are more likely to achieve their goals in a shorter period of time.

As something of an introvert, I was not particularly keen on the idea of self-promotion at first. I wanted my success to be the product of nothing more than the quality of my work, not the result of a solid marketing campaign. What I came to realize is that self-promotion does not have to be shameless, nor does it have to be misleading or dishonest. If you want to achieve sustained success, self-promotion and branding strategies should be transparent, accurate and honest, as this is the best way to begin a relationship with your readers that is based on trust.

Clearly, there is a right way and a wrong way to self-promote, and I will discuss the impact of both in this chapter. There is a fine line between too much and too little, and it can be quite difficult to identify that line. I hope to help you see the line more clearly by addressing the following aspects of self-promotion and branding:

• How to appropriately self-promote
• The influence of branding on potential for growth
• How to take advantage of opportunities to showcase your skills and expertise

Determining an Appropriate Level of Self-Promotion

Remember the issues Homer had with his Internet venture? Of his many mistakes, Homer was guilty of going overboard with self-promotion. Billing himself as the "Internet King," Homer was able to attract a potential client by advertising his services. Unfortunately, he oversold his abilities and could not offer anything of value to the client. As a result, he lost the client. It is not hard to imagine that the prospective client then went on to offer an honest assessment of his experience, thereby ruining Homer's still-developing reputation.

It is always best to promote yourself in a way that is unflinchingly honest. Your readers want to know precisely why they should buy what you are selling, and the only way to do that is to promote your services in the most accurate way possible. Overselling what you are capable of may convince more initial buyers to spend their money, but word will get out quickly and you will have lost the opportunity to win the loyalty of your customers. Showing confidence in your abilities is the clearest path for gaining the trust of the readers who will ultimately buy your products and services.

Branding and Its Clear Influence on Growth Potential

It is undeniably true that branding has a significant impact on the products and services we purchase, as it is almost always the case that -- with all other things being equal -- we will opt for the brand that is more familiar. This extends to blogging as well, which is why it is important to establish a brand identity that can be readily recognized. There are a lot of ways to establish a brand, and it may be as simple as using a catchy name or self-applied title. However you choose to brand yourself, it is important to recognize the impact that your brand will have on growth potential. The appropriate use of branding will help speed the growth of your blog and increase the opportunities for generating profit.

How to Create Opportunities to Showcase Expertise

The most effective way to self-promote is to demonstrate your expertise to a wide audience. Without an established readership, this may seem difficult to accomplish, but it is actually quite easy. Simply identify an established blog that has an audience that you believe would be interested in what you have to say. Guest posts are welcome on most blogs and represent an excellent strategy for attracting an audience of your own. Self-promoting in this way is honest and allows potential readers to get a real sense of what you have to offer.

Some blogs will pay you for your work, while others will actually charge you for the opportunity, but costs or earnings are not what is most important in this instance. Instead, make sure that the audience that will see your post includes the specific type of people that will be most interested in reading more of your work. This will require a bit of research on your end, but taking the time to do so is entirely worthwhile.

Identifying a Central Subject or Concept

If you have already thought about blogging, you have probably already thought about the topics that you would want to address in the online space you create. Even if you have already made a decision on a central subject, it is worth taking a moment to consider the process you used to arrive at that decision. Perhaps you identified a subject that you so thoroughly enjoy that you could not imagine growing tired of discussing it, or perhaps you chose a subject based on its potential for bringing in profit. Maybe the subject you chose is something you are not particularly interested in, but your level of expertise is such that writing at length on the subject would be incredibly simple.

The decision-making process is important when it comes to choosing a central subject, and it is my belief that most people unintentionally adopt a flawed approach. How you arrive at a decision will not preclude you from creating a successful blog, but I think that there are certain aspects that should be prioritized over others, and it is not often the case that new bloggers understand why this kind of prioritization is beneficial.

My advice on this matter is simple: Passion should be the foremost consideration, with adopting a unique approach to the subject being a close second. Of course, this is a highly personal decision, but I think that the advice provided in this chapter will help give you the best chance at succeeding in creating a consistently profitable blog.

Focus on Passion, Not Profit

It is very difficult to fool readers into believing that you are passionate about a subject you do not find interesting. Yet many bloggers choose a subject they don't like simply because they think it will give them the best chance to generate quick and easy profit. While it is true that there are certain subjects in which there are more opportunities to generate passive income than others, it is still the case that you have to develop an interested readership that will be willing to buy your products and services. If you come across as disinterested in your writing, there will not be much of a market for your products and services.

Bloggers who select a topic they are passionate about are much more likely to enjoy the kind of long-term success that can be achieved through passive income strategies. You do not have to be the most knowledgeable or most insightful writer to reap these rewards, as a clear passion for your subject is more than enough to win over a sizable readership.

While this is true, there are also other methods for increasing the likelihood of a subject's success, and taking advantage of these methods is certainly advisable.

Claim an Unfilled Niche

In all likelihood, the subject you are considering writing about has already been covered several times over. This does not mean that you have to abandon your subject to find something that has never been done; it only means that you have to find a novel way of presenting your concept. If plenty of experts have already weighed in on your chosen subject, consider tackling the subject from the perspective of an outsider. If the subject is usually discussed in only broad terms, you can present the narrow view, or you can attempt to link several seemingly disparate subjects so that readers are surprised to see them presented in such a way. Anything that will generate new interest in the subject is worth exploring, and a unique concept or approach can make a significant difference in just how profitable your blog becomes.

Expertise Is Not Necessarily a Prerequisite

One of the biggest obstacles for many would-be bloggers relates to insecurity over their level of expertise. A lack of expertise can actually be a tremendous advantage, as writing from the perspective of someone who has no prior knowledge of a subject often makes the material that much more accessible. Readers relish the opportunity to learn alongside someone who is also new to the subject, and it is much easier to present topics in a lighthearted or comedic way when you are not the world's foremost authority.

For example, I recently decided to take up gardening in an effort to find a new way to occupy some of my free time. While I immediately found blog after blog that offered expert insight into the world of gardening, nearly every blog I read operated from the assumption that I had some prior knowledge or that I knew some of the more basic terminology. It was not until I discovered a blog that documented the experience of someone who was also a total neophyte to gardening that I learned anything of value. There were plenty of posts outlining what not to do and why, with plenty of hilarious stories detailing the kind of embarrassing failures no one else would be willing to share.

Establishing Trust Through Expertise

In order to establish a level of trust that leads readers to confidently buy your products and services, you have to demonstrate that your expertise is valuable. As I mentioned before, you do not have to be a leading scholar on the subject, but you do have to be able to tell customers what it is about the information you possess and the manner in which you present it that makes it worthwhile. Although it may seem like we are entering the realm of salesmanship -- and we are, to a degree -- your ultimate goal is to create a brand that provides outstanding products and services that don't require a "hard sell."

When the readers of your blog are evaluating whether or not to buy one of the products or services you offer, they should feel a clear sense of confidence about what they are getting and whom they are getting it from. If you have been forthright and have accurately demonstrated your expertise, then you are far more likely to enjoy greater sales figures than someone who makes outlandish claims or misrepresents their expertise. So even though you don't need to be a convincing salesperson, you do need to understand the value of each the following traits as they relate to your success as a blogger:

- Transparency
- Honesty
- Continuing education

Value Transparency Above All Else

No one wants to feel like they are being "taken in" or used -- even in some small way -- for someone else's financial gain. One of the more common mistakes made by bloggers is to try to hide some of the products or services they sell, particularly when it comes to affiliate marketing. If you are unfamiliar with these types of programs, many bloggers will write about or recommend a specific product to their readers and then take a percentage of the sales that come from their referrals. Affiliate marketing programs can be quite lucrative, but I believe there is a right way and a wrong way to approach this.

Personally, I only engage in affiliate marketing when it is a product or service I use or am familiar with, and I always let my readers know exactly how I am being compensated. My readers appreciate this approach, and I haven't had any issues with conflicts of interest. Bloggers who aren't transparent in this way may be causing damage to their reputation, and any reader who ends up buying a poor product based on your recommendation will be very unlikely to ever trust your advice in the future.

Be Honest About What You Know and What You Don't

Readers dislike being misled, and there is nothing more damaging for your online blogging business than a poor reputation caused by providing inaccurate or misleading information about yourself, your credentials or your products and services. It is very easy to please your readers when they know what they should expect from you and your blog. If, for example, David Foster Wallace had billed Infinite Jest as a "breezy and simple novel that can be enjoyed in a single afternoon," readers would be outraged when they found out that the book was actually an incredibly complex work of postmodernist literature checking in at over 1,000 pages. Even though many consider Wallace's magnum opus to be one of the most important literary accomplishments of the last 30 years, readers would still be so put off by being misled that they would never bother to read the first paragraph (not to mention the fact that the book would not end up in the right hands, especially since it takes a certain kind of person to want to tackle Wallace's work in earnest).

Gaining Trust Takes Time, But Losing Trust Can Happen in an Instant

It is going to take you some time to build a reputation among your readers, but the trust you engender is always a precariously delicate thing. As I mentioned when discussing affiliate marketing strategies, a single misstep can turn even the most loyal of readers away. You can increase the speed with which you build trust among readers by being consistently honest and forthright, and by doing this you also minimize the likelihood of losing that trust following some unintentional misstep. It should be abundantly clear, however, that intentionally misleading your readers or misrepresenting yourself will turn away most readers on a permanent basis.

Committing to Continuing Education

As someone who is making money from a particular subject, it is absolutely vital that you stay current with any relevant trends and make updates to your blog as necessary. To do this, you have to be committed to continuing to learn about your subject so that you can continue to grow as a blogger. This is especially true if the blog you create is presented from a beginner's point of view, as your initial readers will really enjoy learning and progressing alongside you.

Understanding the Importance of Consistency, Clarity and Quality

There are many traits that all writers seem to share, and perhaps there is none more common than the overwhelming sense of insecurity they often feel about their abilities. This is true of many of the heavyweights of American literature, just as it is true of many of the most lucrative bloggers today. While most people judge their own writing far too harshly, there is a very good reason to be consistently concerned about quality. Your readers will evaluate you based on your ability to write, and even the most valuable information may be summarily dismissed if it is poorly written.

Eventually, you might move on to podcasts, videos and speaking engagements that allow you to clearly communicate with your audience, but until then, your persona and your expertise have to be shared via the written word. This means that you have to be diligent about the quality of your work and careful about the work you choose to publish. You will also have to make conscious choices regarding the tone you use in your writing and how that tone meshes with your particular subject. It is not always the case that certain subjects cannot be presented with a certain tone (many serious academic subjects are tackled with a humorous tone that makes the subject more accessible), but it is important that you maintain consistency.

If you are concerned about your writing skills or feel a sense of insecurity over being published, simply enlist the help of someone to proofread your work before publishing. This is a good practice anyway, but it will help you gain a sense of confidence and identify what aspects of your writing need more work. Of course, it should be obvious that publishing work so laden with errors that it is unreadable will have a disastrous effect on your ability to earn passive income, so take great care in refining your writing skills before moving forward.

Writing Skill and Subject Expertise Are Inextricably Linked

Even though there are many writers who are insecure about what they publish and wind up reading and re-reading what they have written far too many times, there are still others who believe that it is the content of the writing that matters most. This could not be further from the truth. Even the most insightful or innovative ideas will be overshadowed by a lack of basic writing conventions, and readers will quickly judge the intelligence of the author based on their ability to use the written word.

Even Stephen Hawking's work would be dismissed by the overwhelming majority of readers if he routinely made glaring errors that made his work unreadable, so you must understand just how important it is to develop your writing skills so that what you have to say is not overlooked. Of course, this does not mean that you have to be a master of language, only that you have to be able to relay your ideas clearly and in a manner that does not distract from the content.

Style, Consistency and Branding

Your brand encompasses just about everything you do with your blog, and the style of writing you choose will have an impact on the establishment of your brand. You should adopt a style that suits you best and reflects the manner in which you would like to approach your subject. If you feel like you have a flair for humor, then you can take on an informal style that features a comedic take on your subject. If you feel like you should approach your subject with a greater degree of seriousness, then a formal or academic tone would probably work best. Once you have decided upon a tone and style, make sure to remain consistent so readers will develop a sense of familiarity with the way you approach writing.

Lack of Clarity and Impact on Passive Income Potential

The inability to make a point or to help a reader understand the subject you are addressing will have a dramatic effect on your ability to earn passive income. If your writing is inscrutable or requires the reader to repeatedly go over the same sentence just to understand what you are trying to say, then it is very unlikely that you will generate any sort of significant income. Your writing has to be accessible, which means that you have to write in a manner that is clear and, sometimes, incredibly simple. When your writing is accessible, your audience -- and your passive income potential -- is limitless.

Building the Blog and Attracting an Audience

When it comes time to build the actual blog that will become your source of passive income, you will have a lot of decisions to make. The choices you make in the beginning will have a significant impact on the long-term success of the blog, so make sure you take a measured approach before launching the site. Of course, your blog should be an accurate reflection of you and your subject, and you have to remember the influence of perception on your prospective audience. Your blog should look professional and should function well, as you will find it difficult to succeed if the prospective audience judges your site to be amateurish or poorly designed.

There are far too many factors that go into blog building to address in this space, so this chapter will focus on some of the more big-picture issues that play a role in the success of just about every blog regardless of the subject. Though there is no mention of automated transaction systems in this chapter, that subject will be addressed in Chapter 8, which focuses on how and when to monetize your blog. This chapter addresses the key factors that go into the initial building process, including:

- Hosting considerations
- Web design
- Page layout
- Content type
- SEO and other marketing strategies

Again, these are merely the basics of building a blog, but they are also the key components that every blogger should consider as they set up their site. Failing to take these aspects of blog building into account can be disastrous, and while you can accomplish most of these tasks on your own, some projects may require the help of a professional.

Hosting Considerations

One of the more attractive aspects of blogging is the notion that anyone can set one up quickly and free of charge. While there are indeed many free hosting sites that will allow you to set up a very nice blog, the limitations are far too great for you to maximize your earning potential. If you want to be able to customize your site and be able to offer the kinds of products and services that generate passive income, you are going to have to invest in hosting.

While a free site and a hosted site may appear to look similar, you have to realize that a free site puts you at the mercy of the provider, whereas you are in full control of a site that you host yourself. That means you can generate revenue through advertising, change the page layout or site design, and install other options to make the site entirely your own. The cost of hosting is relatively minimal, especially when you consider the freedom that you have in the design and operation of the site.

Web Design and Page Layout

Your site has to look professional for anyone to take you seriously. Any indication of outdated design elements will cast doubt on the value of the products and services you offer, thereby reducing your potential for generating passive income. There are countless design templates that help create the air of professionalism you need for success, and many of these can be easily customized and branded with your specific logos.

If you find yourself completely lost when it comes to web or graphic design, there are many professionals who can assist you at a very reasonable rate. Make sure to look at their portfolio first, and always clearly outline your expectations before entering into any agreement. The site itself should be very easy to navigate and should always focus on directing your readers to the products and services you provide, so make sure the site is designed in a way that is both intuitive and focused on the ultimate goal of generating passive income.

Content Focus

Every blog is going to require updates from time to time, but if your goal is to generate passive income, then you have to focus on creating content that is evergreen. This means that the information in the posts will always be relevant and useful to readers in spite of it being months or years since it was originally posted. Writing blog posts in this way will ensure that there is plenty of valuable content on your site without requiring you to write on a daily basis.

SEO Strategies for Attracting an Audience

Search Engine Optimization, or SEO, is unbelievably important. The majority of your readers will come from an organic search using one of the major search engines, so it is essential that your blog posts appear on the first page of the results. SEO is complicated and ever-changing, so it may be best to enlist the assistance of a professional. Aside from that, guest posts are great ways to drive traffic, and establishing a varied social media presence is also highly beneficial.

Passive Income Explained

Back in Chapter 1, I offered a definition that I believe accurately reflects the concept of passive income. To reiterate, passive income is earned without requiring your presence through the use of automated transaction systems. While this is where the "passive" aspect of the terminology is derived, the process involved in laying a strong foundation can be lengthy and does require some very hard work on your part. Once you get to the point in which your blog is set up with valuable content, products and services, then you can begin to relax and enjoy the passive flow of revenue.

Since we have already introduced the concept of passive income, we can begin to discuss the details that make this an effective strategy, along with the most efficient methods for implementation. In this chapter, I will discuss how to generate passive income while also clearing up some of the most common misconceptions related to the subject. In many cases, aspiring bloggers are attracted to the idea of passive income because of these misconceptions, so it is absolutely critical that you have a thorough understanding of this concept before you proceed.

Why Passive Income?

The beauty of passive income is that it allows you to make an investment with your time rather than selling it off incrementally. The idea is that the hours you spend creating your blog -- along with the products and services you will ultimately offer for sale -- has unlimited potential value, which is typically not the case with a traditional 9-to-5 job. You are paid just once for the hours you work at an office, but passive income allows you to continually profit from the work you have already done.

There are additional benefits as well, as this kind of work gives you greater flexibility with your time. If you are content with your earnings, you can simply enjoy the newfound free time. If you want to improve your earnings, you can just as easily begin another passive income venture, providing you with another opportunity to invest your time up front while creating another potentially unlimited return. If you enjoy freedom and flexibility, then passive income strategies represent an excellent choice.

Common Misconceptions

When most people discuss passive income through blogging, they act as though it is so effortless that anyone can succeed. While it is true that anyone can achieve a phenomenal level of success, it is highly unlikely that it will be easy. As I have mentioned, the products and services you offer have to have value, and you will likely have to update your blog on a regular basis. While blogging for passive income is not effortless, it does represent a more sensible use of time that includes the potential for significant growth and the establishment of financial security. Setting up a successful blog does not happen overnight. You have to take the time to create a valuable brand that will appeal to discerning consumers, especially if you want to generate long-term success. If you invest a lot of time and put a lot of effort into your products and services, you are then much more likely to establish a stable source of passive income that continues to pay off for quite some time.

Strategies and Revenue Streams

In the next chapter, we will talk about some of the most common and most effective strategies for generating passive income, including:

• Advertising
• Affiliate marketing
• Books
• Seminars
• Speaking engagements
• Sponsorships
• Training sessions

As you will see in Chapter 8, some of these strategies

depend on the success of the strategies that precede them. You will also notice that all of these strategies (save for the speaking engagements) do not require your active presence to generate income. That does not mean that you should create a whole suite of video seminars and training sessions before setting up the blog, as you will want to first generate the kind of interest that spurs the demand for those types of products and services. Once the demand is there, you can then create additional products that take audience feedback into account.

Maximizing Potential

It is not uncommon for beginning bloggers to "hedge their bets" when they first start out, and this is somewhat understandable. After all, it is undeniably scary to devote a great deal of time and effort into creating something when there is no guarantee of success. It becomes even more daunting when there are financial costs, but cutting corners at the start will cost you in the long run. If you want to be successful, you have to fully commit to the process. When you act with the possibility of failure in mind, all you are really doing is creating a self-fulfilling prophecy.

When and How to Monetize (Passively!)

Up to this point, we have talked a great deal about the nuts and bolts of blogging as it relates to creating a profitable business through passive income. In doing this, I have mentioned that you have to provide something of clear value to your readers if they are going to make an investment in your products and services, so it should be quite clear that making money is not your only goal in this venture. As someone who is providing insightful and engaging materials, you are actively helping others achieve something that they believe is important, and it is vital that you do not lose sight of that when you come to the point in which it is time to monetize the blog.

My personal advice is to slowly phase in products and services over time. This will allow you to focus on building a core audience that can vouch for the quality of your work over social media, in commenting sections and through other means of referral. This is, of course, not to say that you have to do it this way. Many bloggers begin with products and services available on their site from day one, and this method absolutely works as long as they offer something of clear value. The choice is up to you, but I have always felt that the time invested in engendering a broad sense of trust is ultimately worthwhile.

Plan for Reasonable Expansion

If you plan on monetizing your blog immediately, you should start out by offering just a handful of products and services to your readers. When you design these offerings, make sure that you plan for continued expansion by leaving room for additional products or services that build upon the initial offering. Using a gardening blog as an example, you might begin by offering an eBook that offers beginning gardening tips and then follow that up with intermediate and advanced programs. Eventually, you can develop offerings that are more highly specialized, providing in-depth information on subjects relating to how to grow and care for specific types of plants, or how to maintain a garden in specific hardiness zones.

Of course, these offerings do not all have to be produced using the same medium. If you begin with an eBook that is received well, then you could film a series of videos on the more specialized subjects. Rather than having a set cost per video, you can create a greater perceived value by simply charging for access to the whole set. Depending on your subject, you can also set up other mediums through which you reach your audience, all of which have varying and unique options with regard to monetization. These other mediums will be covered in the next chapter, so for now we will move on to the kinds of products and services you can offer through the blog.

Product and Service Options

As we discussed earlier, you have a great deal of options at your disposal for generating revenue through your blog, including each of the following:

- Advertising
- Affiliate marketing
- Books
- Seminars
- Speaking engagements
- Sponsorships
- Training sessions

When you first launch the site, you may only be in a position to generate income through on-site advertising, affiliate marketing and books. The other options become more viable after the site has become established and is attracting visitors on a regular basis, so your initial focus should be on creating quality content for the site and producing the books that you will offer for sale.

When it comes to advertising, less is always better. Visitors prefer a clean site that is easy to navigate, and filling every available space with advertising is a sure way to alienate your potential audience. Besides, your main revenue streams will be through the actual products and services you offer, so don't go overboard with ads. Once you are established and the site is generating your target income through product and service sales, I suggest eliminating the advertising altogether, or at least opting for a single banner ad.

Once your books and training sessions begin reaching your audience and are being received well, you can start hosting large online seminars that include other experts as well. Depending on whether you want to really leverage your blog's success, you can also offer in-person speaking engagements, but -- especially since we are discussing passive income opportunities -- it is always best to record these in-person sessions so they can be sold on the site and used again in the future.

Expanding Reach Through Additional Mediums

Successful blogging is all about building an audience. After all, the best way to maximize your potential for passive income is to reach as many people as possible. There is a sort of snowball effect that occurs over the course of this process, as you gain more and more momentum as your audience becomes larger and larger. The hard part, however, is getting that snowball rolling to the point where you no longer have to give it any sort of push, and that is best achieved by utilizing several different mediums through which you can reach more people who will be interested in what you have to offer.

While we have already discussed affiliate marketing in earlier chapters, it is helpful to note the reason why companies are eager to offer commissions to bloggers who write about their products. The concept is simple, as these companies are simply trying to reach consumers who might not be exposed to the traditional mediums in which companies tend to advertise. As a blogger, you should consider this approach as a blueprint for expanding your audience. Through the use of a variety of different mediums, you are much more likely to build an audience that values what you have to say and wants to learn more.

SEO strategies are still of paramount importance in driving traffic to your site, but the following mediums should also be considered as a means for building your audience:

• Social media platforms (Twitter, Instagram, Facebook, Google+, etc.)
• Podcasting
• Video channels

Even if you are not familiar with each of these mediums, it is worth learning how to use each one for the purpose of generating more traffic to your site.

Social Media

A surprisingly large portion of the population uses social media for getting the bulk of their information on a daily basis, and with good reason. It is often the case that all of the most recent news is posted to Twitter or some other platform first, and users are able to quickly look at their feed for the information they find relevant to their personal interests.

As a blogger, you have to take advantage of social media by establishing a presence on each platform, especially since the user demographics tend to vary. Depending on your target audience, you may want to heavily focus on Instagram rather than Facebook, or vice versa. To ensure the broadest possible reach, I suggest establishing an active, useful and entertaining presence on as many platforms as possible.

Podcasting

Podcasting is an increasingly important medium, and you do not have to have a studio or a soundboard to create a podcast. At minimum, starting a podcast only requires a microphone, a computer and audio editing software. Depending on your computer, you may not need to buy any equipment at all, though it is advisable to consider an audio interface, a portable XLR recorder and pop filters.

A podcast on its own is not likely to generate any direct revenue at first, as you have to have an audience that listens to your podcast on a regular basis before you can attract advertisers and sponsors. While generating income through the podcast is something of a process, your initial goal is to drive additional traffic to your blog, which makes it a worthwhile endeavor right from the start. Over time, you can monetize the podcast while continuing to generate interest in your blog and in the products and services you offer.

Video Channels

The most popular video platform is still YouTube, and there are countless channels that have millions of subscribers. The revenue generated through advertising alone can make these channels incredibly lucrative, and there is the added benefit of being able to quickly bring in additional audience members. Of course, the advertising revenue represents yet another form of passive income, and there are many people who prefer to access information through a video format rather than a written one.

There are other reasons to use video as well, since a YouTube channel is a great place to post samples of the videos and training sessions that are for sale on your website. You can direct visitors to the site to watch the first video in a series available for sale, and if the visitor feels the first video contains the kind of valuable information they are seeking, they will probably go on to pay for access to the videos that follow. Since you will be offering information provided through audio, video and the written word, you will be able to meet the needs of a diverse audience that possesses varied preferences.

Leveraging Expert Status to Generate Added Opportunities

Just as an audience grows at an exponential rate, the same is true of the opportunities that will be at your disposal once you have established a popular, revenue-generating blog. Having a core audience that trusts you and is willing to follow your advice is a powerful form of currency, and you may wish to leverage that currency by seeking out additional methods for bringing in profit.

The loyalty of your audience is more than enough to prove your expertise as it relates to your chosen subject, so you will find that your newfound status as an expert can lead to speaking invitations and consulting opportunities, among other things. Some of these opportunities are not necessarily passive in nature, but there are some very good reasons to accept an invitation to be a featured speaker or to work in a consulting role. In terms of growth potential and the expansion of your reach, these sorts of opportunities are outstanding.

Of course, your goals may be quite simple, and if you want to achieve a sustainable source of passive income so that you have ample time to enjoy life, then these opportunities may not be worth the initial cost in time. Personally, I believe these options to be more than worthwhile, as accepting these opportunities can help you achieve the kind of success that ultimately leads to complete financial security. Remember, the goal of passive income is to make investments of time early on that continue to pay off, and leveraging your status as an expert in this way is an investment of time that can yield a significant return.

Speaking Engagements

As I mentioned, there are many successful bloggers who avoid these sorts of engagements because their goal was to earn passive income, and a speaking engagement requires their active presence. While that is certainly true, it is important to recognize that you are still in full control of the value of your time, so set a price you believe is fair and don't ever feel obligated to accept an invitation to speak.

Even though your active presence is required for a speaking engagement, it does not mean that it is not possible to use the engagement to generate passive income. Not only are you reaching a new audience, solidifying your reputation and reinforcing your brand by doing so, but you can also record the lecture so it can be posted to your video channel or included as part of a video series for sale on your website.

Consulting

Consulting is another opportunity that becomes available once you achieve a certain level of success in blogging about your particular subject. You can offer a fixed price for consulting services right on your website, or you can simply wait for unsolicited requests to trickle in. If you are good at what you do, you will not have to work hard to generate consulting opportunities.

Unlike speaking engagements, however, there are not that many ways to turn a consulting gig into a source of passive income. I tend to avoid consulting requests, not because I do not wish to offer my assistance to anyone who asks, but rather because I believe the products and services I offer are more than sufficient. If one of my readers still has a question or requires clarification on a subject, I don't mind freely providing it as quickly as possible. This policy also allows me to update my products and services based on the types of questions I am asked, which helps me ensure that my materials are as comprehensive as possible.

Guest Posts and Seminars

When you first start out as a blogger, guest posts are a necessary means for attracting an initial readership, but that is not the only instance in which a guest spot is valuable. With the benefit of a large readership, other blogs and websites that want to attract a larger audience often turn to established bloggers to write a guest post. These posts can be quite lucrative, and they serve a dual purpose by sending new readers to the site on which they are posted and further solidify your reputation as an expert in your field.

Seminars are another way that bloggers can collaborate with each other, and there are significant benefits to hosting an online seminar that is streamed live and recorded for future use. With several experts included in the seminar, the perceived value is significant, and a seminar represents an opportunity to create a new set of beneficial products to be sold on your site. Everyone involved in the seminar benefits, and it is an excellent way to achieve another source of passive income, especially since those who attended the live session will be able to vouch for the quality of the seminar.